© 2016 by Lois Shaw. All rights reserved.
Published by Vantage Point Publishing
Indianapolis, IN 46205

No part of this publication may be reproduced or transmitted in any form or by any means, electronic or mechanical, including photocopy, or any information storage and retrieval system, without permission from the publisher. The only exception is a brief quotation in printed reviews.

Limit of Liability/Disclaimer of Warranty: While the publisher and author have used their best efforts in preparing this book, they make no representations or warranties with respect to the accuracy or completeness of the contents of this book and specifically disclaim any implied warranties of merchantability or facilities for a particular purpose. No warranty may be created or extended by any persons. The advice or strategies herein may not be suitable for your situation. You should consult with a professional where appropriate. Neither the publisher nor author should be liable for any loss of profit or any other incidental damages, including but not limited to special, consequential, or other damages.

This is a work of fiction. Names, characters, businesses, places, events and incidents are either the products of the author's imagination or used in a fictitious manner. Any resemblance to actual persons, living or dead, or actual events is purely coincidental.

ISBN 978-1-943159-08-06

Library of Congress Control Number: 2017905829

The publisher would appreciate notification where errors occur so that they may be corrected in subsequent printing and/or editions. Please send comments to the publisher by emailing to deeprivers67@yahoo.com

Printed in the United States of America

Walking in the Spirit

by

Lois Shaw

Welcome to, "Walking in The Spirit" a book of poems created as I walk my life journey guided by the Spirit of God. My poetry is unique in delivery, representing the essence of my spiritual self that accompanies me every waking hour. I like to understand my work as prophetic writings for it is my profound believe that the Poets of today are the later day prophets with messages ordained of God to distribute what the Spirit has released unto them. I am not a typist, yet when I am heart engaged in my writings, my hands fly across the keys with a minimum of error as my mortal man interprets that my Father ordained for me to release into the earth, in my spiritual poetry. I am excited to share in addition a few collaborations in this writing, that were birthed with my collaboration Poet, Mr. Jeffery A. Sanders Sr. the author of "Chapters". Prayers go forth that each word be encouraging, uplifting and a blessing in the life of each reader.

    Lois Shaw

Acknowledgments

   First and foremost, I give thanks and Glory to God for trusting me with this assignment and certainly I believe He is most pleased. My love blankets my family who encouraged me and believed strongly in my work, but there is always the exception to the rule, thank you cousin Tiffany Carter for your encouraging flow of words in my dark hours, bless you. I smile at my sister and brother who too encouraged I move as God said move, Shirley and James, thank you. Last but never least my collaboration Poet who always had another verse of hope to share with me, Jeffery A. Sanders Sr. I thank you with eternal love for being in place to be used by Father. This has been a beyond awesome time, I verbal it cosmic. One love to life.

Lady of Love

From the Author …. From the weight of my pen flows the essence of my spirituality and love. In my writings, I speak tirelessly of both for they are kin. Lady of Love is my performing and pen name that I wear proudly as I scribble on blank canvass the language of my spirit and my love, the blessings of my calling I share graciously with each of you.

Table of Content

Poem 1   Blessed

Poem 2   Beloved

Poem 3   My Solomon

Poem 4   Can I Blame time

Poem 5   Chariots and Bloom

Poem 6   Close my Space

Poem 7   Cosmic Glance

Poem 8   Did Not Her Crown Tilt

Poem 9   He gave a Smiling Nod

Poem 10   Light and Knowledge

Poem 11   Listen to the Rain

Poem 12   Love is Whole

Poem 13   Love Talking

Poem 14   Mental Purification

Poem 15   Vespers

Poem 16   Spiritual Powers Bring Us   Collaboration

Poem 17   Free

Poem 18   Grand Manifestation

Poem 19	Had to Encourage Myself
Poem 20	Halls
Poem 21	He Knows
Poem 22	He Took Me Higher
Poem 23	Her Verbal Pen
Poem 24	High Levels
Poem 25	Higher Thought
Poem 26	The Princess and the Prince of the Royal Secret Collaboration
Poem 27	How do I Sisterhood with You
Poem 28	How it Feels
Poem 29	I feel it All the Time
Poem 30	I Hear His Voice
Poem 31	Cosmic High
Poem 32	In My Soul
Poem 33	Intelligence is Spiritual
Poem 34	Over the Trod Collaboration
Poem 35	Knowledge in His Halls
Poem 36	Natural Queen
Poem 37	Next Time

Poem 38	Not a Minute More	
Poem 39	On Destiny Road	
Poem 40	His Love	
Poem 41	A Breeze	
Poem 42	Beauty is Her Thought	
Poem 43	Eternal Love	
Poem 44	Either	
Poem 45	Hear the Truth	Collaboration
Poem 46	Wake Up Shake UP	
Poem 47	Mental Seed	
Poem 48	Redeemed	
Poem 49	Positive Thoughts	
Poem 50	Revelation	
Poem 51	Scholar	Collaboration
Poem 52	The Whole Seal	
Poem 53	Three Witness	
Poem 54	Walk in the Light	
Poem 55	Walk om Dust	
Poem 56	Love is no Mystery	
Poem 57	If I were Rich	

Poem 58   How Real Is   Collaboration

221 BLESSED

BY

Lady

When I think of Your goodness my soul cries Hallelujah Praise your Holy Name...I could have been lost or dead in my sins...but I received your sacrificial blood offering for me... I am so blessed and highly favored of You Precious Savior...You never left my side...there were times I walked in silence as Your loving hand guided me around the many dangers toils and snares that I stand to testify how you lead me all around each and every one...Right there I put ...thank you...

The snares I know today were for my test to teach the lessons of my gained experiential degree ...I tore the fabric of my heart... but praise You Father your Eternal love mend, Reinforced and solidified every fiber and placed a whole heart and a right spirit within this earthen vessel... Lord I praise You...

I have encountered many afflictions and dis appointments that would have toppled most and some more...each and every one you lifted me out of them...

With your mighty hand and the total of my faith in You...

In my distress you quickly hear my cry and your Love seals every leak …. Fortifying whole ….Bless you loving Father...

I shed tears of joy for in You I find the greatest of all Loves and you have taught me the tenants and constitution of Agape love….

I adore you Adonai the Everlasting Arm of Eternal Love…

You instructed let that offended spirit die quickly…

And with me it can't live long…God help me to teach this the more…I bow my head in your presences Holy One and worship you…

©

Ls

Beloved

Lady ©

She came on to his shores in the summer of his October bringing with her an excitement that delighted his artistic charm… he was taken by her mysterious manner but knew it to be the substance that made her so sexy to him in so many ways…he saw her as "reconnected to his spiritual realm man…" adorning her with prose uttered from his floral arrangement… perfumed in his spectacular verbal accentuation of his expressed love for her…

Light from her soul reflected in his mirrored gaze as light opened the path of darkness claiming the dark for her own lighted space…she lingers in his soul not in a rush but softly penetrating the layers bringing sweet nectar of her pure heart to cushion every thrusting blow from life …

Her quiet spirit caused apprehension in small millimeters on his intellectually conscious sphere…remedy summoned his trust, reminding him of their committed commune that was birth in sacredness upon a much different geometric more complex than common mathematics…she laid bare before him as did he without natural voice for the mental surrender of his consonants spoke to her personally…

She saw him eons ago nestled and calm in her infra- red solutions...his scent married her soul ...she taste him as drifts of breeze bears his un corruption she holds him ever so closely...

I watched you look into my eyes as if what you saw in my soul would vanish... concentration on what you know has parted your silent lips approaching her from your cosmic arch...

Smiles erupt in my skyline from my sexy thoughts of you...for our carnal baptism is lofty...our instruments of application are flesh that transcends time and commands space expanded her area for we...we have lived multiple orbits to find the charters of our loving unison not formed by the chapters and dictates of contamination...alas my dear love we linger deep in posture of eternal love from it we came forth ...

Ls

©

My Solomon

Lady of Love

I heard your voice bring my soul to you seated on your throne she sat in submission to his truth…it may seem impossible to those who dwell not in the spirit …heard your confident laughter reminding of your fierce statement that requested agreement from me I obliged for the science of exchange allows you to capture the audience of my mind be it in the physical or telepathy…after a few lines of encounter stacked shelves formed as we shared truth in understanding forming another level…

I spoke a volume without hesitation desiring you speak to my heart…I liquidated control for your complex rules of exponent information which logical repetition brought about sufficient surety building our foundation of convinced…

It gets so deep sometimes I must kiss you resuscitating she to digest your elaborate literature …each day you spread a banquet table for my mental consumption …so waiting for that long debate and when it's done, ooo wee….only a man that can stimulate her mind holding her in ecstatic captivity can dessert with her in those succulent and lavish ways…

Let me sweep over your statue like balmy breezes on the beach… allow my hair to cover your bareness as we rock ourselves into atmospheric pressure changes, changing your dry climate to wet ...let me refresh you with an offering of raisins from Kedar let his energy replenish like lightning streaking the midnight sky ...only he who has dwelled in the energy of Creation a second time is worthy...let her move the elderberry bush from your path a limb at a time...as you cradle me in your love ...I linger on the tear in your eye desiring to change it to clear flowing joy...hold me my darling I will hold you forever ... whisper into my soul products of distant shores as your wise unfolds the meaning... 10302015

Ls

©

Can I Blame Time

Lady of Love ©

I looked at myself beside myself…I started a conversation
With time …for it will be he who will definitely walk
Through time with me to the gates of eternity…I felt maybe I
Have spent to much of his value on situations and people who
Had no measure to help me or even care for real about me…

Time, do I apologize for the vast waste of you…
When I study my journey …I think it wasted not
For every step as I reflect was a course of learning
And growth…Information gained is worth
More than any amount of treasure …
Wisdom applied to my library of wise
Can't be extracted and made null…
Personal, growth there is no compare

I am where I should be on the Highway of Life time
I may have had some pause and delay…
I needed that for deep excavation for knowledge
Sake …Seek and ye shall find …I sought
I found …this has been add to my information
Center supporting as I teach among my beloved,,,

The delays are what I want to reconcile with time
Time waved me forward…
I trod on… there is non to reconcile …

There are some glorious things I feel deep within the
Center of my soul… Time is refraining my
Forward motion on it …I tried to rise into
The cosmic atmosphere where there is no space nor
Time and was rebuked in and for the human push

I'm almost confused…My issue lies within my
Instant gratification that was the fuel that
Wasted the time I speak …Oh let my heart sing ..
Hush not my song of love…yet there is so much more

I realized it was my selfish speaking…
My God has been so good to me
I should be dead …but He saw fit to use me
My testimony is in my spoken word
I may have a message that may speak to flesh
But that is the temple that houses the spirit that governs the
Precious dirt house…
Oh to rescue me from the lot of instant… I know I
Can make it…my Glorious walks with me until
It's that time…

Ls: LoL
©

Chariots and Blooms ©

By

Lady of Love ©

The scented love of my exceptional blooming garden met your empty and broken... at the west end...

The hint of strong desire in truth began a thaw in your ice chest...

There was never a mental incarcerated lecture from the bottom or top...I saw the fear in you lip...as you tried to hid the view of your real concern...I adopted this faulty trend and adjudicated in behalf of you...

This is a Chariot...

My weakness was made strong for the purposes to come... precious value of meet, definition would pave this forward path...the vow of loyalty held her head high as the crowning of your approval met the standard of receptions quality...

I saw the motivational balance swing equal for both...as the sun of many meditations shown high and wide in an eastern sky...

Her cosmic swing kept vigil of each page as turned ...the temptation to... never out weighs the assignments placed in our hands...as the eagerness replaces the broad of slack...

I sought the rose of tender and placed her at your feet

As she ministered to your stones ...the bright path of constant opened the right side of her gate... could you not readily feel the breeze of a million deserts at night?... each wave brought living testimony to encourage the parts attempting to turn ghost ...

You see the evidence of eternal life ...

This is the Bloom...

Ls

©

Close My Space...03272015 ©

By

Lady

I walked into your late hour... the bridge that supported my travel was the one to continue to support the near forward motion...

The bright and loving star that guided my flight kept me in a protective shield...

Did he witness the last motion of her focused arrival...

Or was he still caught up in mental psychology of his on method and natural kind...

Let my prophecy on the tenant of this known journey ...

The land will become over run with mass hysteria...the foundations that stood as monuments in your life will dissolve in a matter of moments as though vats of acid had poured like rain over their foundations... the close of your covered valley will open as to swallow your local misery...then will the nightingale shrill her tune...and the roses bloom in the moon of the sun ... there shall be the garden of and arranged ornament displayed for your now cordial obedience...

I fell in silence till the scent of this new wind had passed...

On the soft of my shoulder you rest an inquiring hand… my response was to continue this amazing assignment… seeing it to the end…

Your eyes studied my motion and shroud your head

As I pulled my tallit closing my space for prayer…

LS

©

Cosmic Glance

Lady©

I felt your mind walk thru the door of my thoughts bringing your presences before me…gracing my mind with declared wisdom as his soul embraced my heart… seating his verbal purpose to address her central understanding…speaking to the sensitive realm of my heart and strengthen the valley landscape…let your adoring contribute his floral arrangement along her satin path enriching her garden with new buds…bringing to life seed planted from that far age…I in the telepathic strength of hearing understood this lesson as it escaped your silent lips, would require my frequency elevation ….she secured it without delay …I was excited and swallowed hesitation that would diminish my vision…

Early morning brings with her vision and needed instructions…

You spoke to me soul not my mind as we entered the fourth gate baptizing in the spiritual waters of the moon and the astrological marker of cancer coming forth from the dripping waters with pearls of wisdom woven in our hands given to us from ancient prophecy for distribution in the foreign land…

Great responsibility to impart the truth from the third door reinforcing sudden and sure destruction rest in tampering with the sacred things of God …

Ls

©

Did Not Her Crown Tilt ©

By

Lady ©

The fragrance of our love scented the air...with the charm of magnolia and lavender ... this effect on my senses may be caused by the tantalizing adore of our mental spiritual fusion... Have the ripples of passion ever danced in elaborate array as they do today in your soul...Your thoughts teach my thoughts of every changing facet ... as your left hemisphere patients for its fill from the cosmic range willfully sought by you to exercise prudent care of the city in your care ...See I feel these things... astrologically I discovered why ... which has been become a prominent level to rest my spirit and soul on...

As my journey forwards ...your wise instructions are thru subjected verbs and clear metaphoric slides ... some may find a bit unsettling ...this out pour increases my inner bounty enabling me to produce multiple fruits from my spirit ...the reason for these procedures are because of the spiritual content ...It appears fleshy but the tangible can only be obtained from a mental prescription a spiritual encounter...

My eastern chart carried so many dialects of the obfuscates that were convoluted to most which rang clear as a bell to me...I proceeded on those odd days to whisper the intelligence of our order and the complete of our separate stanzas... the crystal anointing validated this promise... not with the marks of flesh ... the light never goes out...

The wilderness varied in degrees of agreement ...when I would feel this void... your love of soothe turned the muddling fog to sunshine...and scented it with the roses of your mastermind verbs...

These tenants of your heavenly subjects...were discussed in the Citadel of much concern...which brought tones of actual mental conflict to that which understood not...

The love was never physical... it was ordained form the foundation ...baptized in sacred love and will have life...

I can only speak the tribute of truth...as my gratitude tilts her crown...

Ls

©

He Gave A Smiling Nod....06152015 ©

Lady ©

Was this easy for you ...you gave the approving nod and smile... maybe the ease stems from your physical absence...

Is he the one...baby... I already know...

The hall of mirrors reflected the wide continent of his intelligentsia as it spilled into the oceans of his wisdom ... washing the shores with influenced foundations of truth ...

To the acute of hearing... and the advent seekers...

I knew it was him before your awaited nod of smiling approval...

My other observation was the dignitas of his moral character... for sure the rudiment of him I've been privileged to acquaint with as I leisurely referenced his moral psychology from the inlaid chapters he carries deep in his side... and found the pillar firm and just...

The middle village was his proving ground ...as the structures of his enormous formed at the feet of his Gamaliel ...east of the garden ...under the willow of the Bohdi near the winds of Sinhalese...there the mastery was imparted sanctifying the message from the foundation …making the combinations palatable to the masses…

I saw a great and ugly beast use the cloak of night to devour the instructions of the guided prophet …he feared not the controlling spirit of the foul beast and continued the much needed journey …

The text of his language re formulated his science and gained technical knowledge …his wisdom calculations modulated as like the changes that regulate the music of a beautiful song…I heard his thoughts echo in his library and prepared to assist in the trod…on the ring I saw a golden key …representing this is legal and regal …As he gave a smiling nod…

Ls

Light and Knowledge
By
Lady of Love

I awakened in a charged atmosphere that captured my attention
Of course my natural practice began her relay of busy,,,
My inner self was in the presences of the spirit of God …
He was calling for change in my worship …
He said my hands must be clean and my heart pure
Nor my soul given over to vanity
He warned of the pits from swearing deceitfully …
What is this mystery that you have placed in my
Inner sanctum …?
This metaphoric impartation was not of complicate as
It may have appeared complex…
I busied my continue and there rose the sign
Of a prophet that had returned as an in depth. with voice
Of concern and warn …

He left the chart in plain view …my concentrate afflicted
My desire was to engage in a different atmospheric hall
I tended the scroll thrice …my reply to the prophet
Elevated me to a cosmic realm of promised
Lighted dawn…
There appendage a small resistance
Michael fought the lingered tail …
I peered in the higher heaven to receive the new, a glorious
of born…

A dirt inhabitance in forward trod realizing at the connecting rode
I lingered a bit to long…I found the gold laid by. told of old, and
Reoccurred the information, to solidify that I am sure…
This mornings impartation secured for me two generous things…

I know this requires renewal of spirit, entering the Temple gates
To meditate, but not in ritualistic tones .. the script of regulation
Has been so unclearly divided …
The divide was separation from the nauseam of this life's vicissitudes
To connect and restore and revitalize my energy flow…
The next was of a personal order …I was satisfied with the Classification and evaluation …both were in order…
I continue for the better of my servitude in humble robes
And a heart of glad tidings …
Ashe …Ashe

Ls/LoL

Listen To The Rain 10072015

Lady©

The earth is responding in harmony and obedience to God of Universal Creation ...I hear her voice echoing warnings from her deep pockets in her bosom... her mathematical formation is sacred as she ponders the lack of observance from the tribe of dust...she acrobats the storms and whispers in the wind judgment is close on our human horizon ...do we continue to forward into destruction or wise to the voice of truth ...wake up oh ye inhabitants and hear the truth of the Lord...

Prophetic utterance has been sold like supermarket items in violation of the freedom of truth... a remnant is assembled armed with truth from wise study as instructed to show approval of all delivered words in holiness ...sacred ancient text opened minds creating wise verbal construction ...intense in content bringing vital clarity to misinterpretations and entertaining rhetoric...sitting in the quiet of my meditating thought I'm prompt to say , " listen wisely to the rain"...

I sat on the outer perimeter watching the elite of a servitude leave their first estate and sew their garments with reflections of an earthly temporal crown as they spewed a lope sided logic lifting up a man who lain a spiritual guilty blanket across the blinded eyes and minds of human sheep ...are we all like sheep ears tuned to the voice of the wrong Shepard...listen to the rain...

Set in among you are the voices of much wisdom ...as their overload of spontaneous sometimes shaking you to attention pours over the lines of your mental composition tablet yet you take not wisdom of isolation to absorb informative knowledge building up yourself to effectively stand armed against half-truth and uncertain traditional recitations ...you let the poison drip of naysayers infiltrate you intuitive posture rendering you weak and unresponsive to the taps at your third eye door... did not Jude inform you from his text what you would be faced with ,..the description of the master deceiver and his tactics of infiltration are plain ….the sacred script of truth touched by filthy hands of hierarchy that you worship...many of you desire to rise in degrees of sure damnation not realizing nor have you studied to find God's approval for your life...

Burdened with convoluted thought sitting on traditional benches listening to what ...for real you really don't know...I submit from the truth of my knower to not be as sheep in that you march blindly to the slaughter...the conduct of sheep parable is that your demeanor be as sheep but own wise ears to the voice of truth ...take no thought that the messenger is a remnant...the elite cloth has been torn and sewn into its fabric is the textile of the prince of the air ...when your vision clears you will see...but for now ...listen to the rain...

Ls

Love Is Whole... 04022915

By

Lady ©

The angelic beauty of your words captivated my mind not as to imprison my thought... but the pause was to identify the expressions of your majestic presences...

Your vocal wave rest in my inner ears soul from the first combination of notes ...as your spirit turned samples into a broad symphony ...dialing into my heart knowing the answer from the mirror of my soul...you softly rest your roses against my breast as your arms secure the pure loving motions of your heart...

Loved, let me stay here with you...I am so comfortable...the tranquility of this amazing peace has moved those gray shadows that tried to bring a chill to your hearth of exquisite love...

Soft are the petals of each verb... your metaphoric range has me in awe...as your wisdom brings the instructions to support your undaunted love applied to the whole of my soul...

I was in the halls of extreme delight when I heard your opening phrase of whole love...there has been a living gap between the last whole verb and now...my soul lifts her hand to unite with you on this mental stage... as we execute syllable and phrase into patterns of harmony...made for the chorus of our united souls ... touching whole with whole...recognizing whole...

Ls

©

Love Talking

By

Lady

May I talk to love....

One of those lazy days as you drift into my mind as if you were taking a stroll in the park of my thoughts...I wondered had you come to plant a priceless row in my spiritual garden igniting wisdom that storms have no power to blow away...

Before my night journey I viewed a passage that tried to attach its self to my journey...I know the intent upon the evil onset was a design from darkness...blessings of richness came to balm my mini bruise and promote healing for my continued journey...In this door I opened... I openly rebuke myself...

Healing for my in the natural and the spirit is not a drawn out measure....my love for love witness to me in sincere intervals... keeping our communications sacred...I would at times I could open that part of me with you... as my honesty brings revelations...I sense the cry of your concern... you are there with me ...wisdom has bound the urgency to play a more passive role to allow the softest realm to bring out my uneasiness and calm it to silence from your core of real ... you have the same measure of uneasiness ...I admire your strong approach to a natural concern given the elements of our sometimes distance...

Ls ©

Mental Purification
By
Lady ©

It was a simple conversation that turned to learning sharing moments…amazing to say the least…my spirit of discernment rest with her eyes and ears open on a different frequency than the one I left to gather at this juncture…

The intensity of our verbal distribution filled the air above blocking negative intentional entry …we were both aware the information exchange affirmed our present sacred knowledge while agreeing our verbal emissions flowed in sacred wisdom gathered on separate paths but the same journey …

My heart opened wide her door of compassion as her womb seemed to allow a reentry all though it would only be for healing… my natural mother was summoned… I knew I was Divinely chosen to care for this task as my companion delivered messages and revelations stored in safety…I looked at the source with an eye of curiosity to hear a tell tale echo which found no residence in our communicating parcel …stocked with orated knowledge exchange drifting in and out of the large triangle association… deep set in our history that has cornerstone half truth with un holy substitutes hiding the strict mathematics of a peoples mental freedom… brought me to the reason I expelled a word of truth not long before in my blood line ….my verbal companion and I shared the same snare at the ignorance of the unlearned operating in the sphere they claimed expert knowledge of…
They worked among the twisted and tampered scriptures with a pride of deceit to harvest their own selfish gain… they are so rooted in the foolery they themselves believe the lies ….it angered these fake peddlers of altered truths…

causing them to label our protected minds against the lies as demonic inspired…so sad …

I'm now awake as so much dances on my mental screen giving my mind electric boosts… elevating my understanding as these facts continue to appear causing me to literally take notes… for my spiritual lantern burned a holy scent flooding my acute attention …study to show thy self approved rings in my ears… this is what they haven't done…using information taught by those who have corrupt sacred word for the purpose of controlling a nation of people…

Ls
© 09132015

Vespers

By

Lady of Love

In my solitude...rang a song familiar in word an tune

In my spirit...the words ...When morning glides the

Skies...My heart awakens cries...May Jesus Christ be Praised...

                                                            J. Barnby

Strange I pondered...Morning... its evening near...

The message was not for the physical dawning...the message

Reveled awareness of life's steps and lessons learned has now

Become our mental morning... Out of clear understanding and acceptance

Of profound revelation... be it individual or community

My heart (Mind) awakens my (our) eyes come open.,.. that lesson

Has been reveled and the scales of blindness have fallen away

...

May the Lord Be Praised... Divine revelation

Ls/Lol

©

7/13/14

Spiritual Power Brings Us

Jeffery/Lois

As we awaken… we tend our faults… fears and difficulties… Our limitations and selfishness on the path… we shall find rude awakenings… Spiritual power brings us together. An affair of walking together faithfully. Spirituality is that power that brings us to the threshold of the undertaking…..

When we walk after the spirit, we mind not the things of flesh...We are aware of our dirt house... But the spirit is the governor of what manifest in the flesh be it of God or satan...

She speaks from a strong position; don't worry about the inner homework. It has been done in Spiritual attainment, not an esoteric knowledge. But a study of great texts and sutras and Systematic learning in a deep rich searching, as so it stems from the abundant…Wisdom of the heart…

Now we must be mindful to try the spirit. Meaning test it to see if it be clear or altered by,
A multitude of convoluted chatter...my dear friend Difficulties are a life time in the dirt house...

Yet how can many do so, when they are confused by their bestial spirit that makes one seek the realm of control and power, when they are not taught to test the spirit, but receive shaded eyes and Words to just sit still and obey, being a slave as though the blind continues To lead the blind, still thinking the world is flat line; I would think. The lost still think so, when their lives lay flat. Will they ever become enlighten, or stuck in the everyday reminding of staying spiritually, mentally sleep.

The Divine Spirit gives us smooth exits from trials. When we are free will students and practitioners of His knowledge, when we know this we walk equally yoked...Not in bondage, but as a valuable unit of information and instructions!!

Then those who walk the walk into the light. Those who have greeted

their true spirit within Sense the simple loving Presence in each moment, be aware of how the spiritual life can guide us towards this. Every ancient system of wisdom teaches us, that spiritual and human life unfolds in
A succession of stages evolving cycles of honor in the right of passage, that all Spirituality's full consciousness in the seasons of inner grace…

Exactly Grand Major...We were spirit first before dirt... That spirit is a constant loving, Teaching and a positive guide... The voice of Him comes from the prime seat in your knower... To capture the full essence or to receive the uttering of His loving teaching, you must acquaint your ear inn your knower with his beautiful voice!!...Living in the stream of His guidance is bliss... Yes it comes in growth stages...As lesson is learned; you ascend to higher heights and deeper depths, Living within your dirt house!!

What happens in the meditation…? Helps us to participate in the marketplace, Without attachment, realizing everything is in your spiritual practice, Change comes

to our lives, not only from shifts of our inner need, But also from shifts in our external circumstances, The nature of our existence is ceaseless transformation, We must respect the changing cycles that life brings and accept The inner task of our spiritual growth rhythms without being,
Adolescence to them……

The mediation made us aware of the pitfalls that could abort our mission...The market place or the arena, if I may change the verbal directional course Has been visited over the clicks of time, by both and we have circulated Shallow and deep therein... We are not unlearned of these things...Attaching to unsuitability is like sudden death of our mission!!The infusion of our spirit is not carnal in origin it is of the spirit.

Adult life brings its own spiritual task and openings, Many will bring it to mere carnality, without thinking…We have responsibility to develop passionate concern, Who cares what others who have yet to experience ripened life, The fruit of

spirituality have in thought and wayward speech,
we have the right to fulfill our own unique expressions, unfortunately we will disreguard them in their little splendid periods of wandering in denials, who masquerade in false spiritual realization? If they look at themselves they still can't see, each day they break the rules of their bible…Take the log out of your own eye, before you judge your brother, that's why I am still and
Let them live behind the walls of their own harden hearts…because my own solitude, Makes me aware of problems I will encounter, as well as the difficulties, enjoying the reflections,
Seeing their stories as an adventure, appreciating its cycle and turn with a sense of wonder and gratitude, Feeling myself rest in the wonder of the day with the openness toward my life ahead…

The openings to the path of spiritual knowledge are cut in intervals of ten clicks Major... Every ten clicks you either grow in knowledge from the lesson learned in That interval or you stand to repeat the cycle again ...thus retarding your

maturity To fit you for it at the next interval...The carnality is a sign of immaturity, A sign of lesson or lessons unlearned....when you are able to control the flesh, By bringing under subjection to what has been taught to you in the Spirit...Genuine passion and compassion will never be hidden behind a mask of religiosity or Harden tricky hearts...I agree my solitude provides a knowing ground. .
It has taught me to be prudent, not arrogant...at times a bit firm...Teach Major….

What mega city in verbal word display, Mature responsible and committed,
Click, click and click again, Yet seasoned adventurer in the cycle of patience,
In sacred place that inspire you, the honor of her choices that rest on her resources,
Did she say genuine passion and compassion, the nearest enemy of compassion is pity,
Which is a still born separation; yes I too with you share the sorrows of life,
But what of those who are the enemy of Sympathetic joy,

when they of other people only see comparison, which looks to see if we have more of
The same. The same as other or less than another? Instead of rejoicing with them,
And so we have to teach them that the enemy of equanimity is indifference,
True equanimity is balance, and indifference is withdrawal…..

Wise one because we have been taught to cry and Lift up the down trodden and rejoice
When good fortune falls to our brother...we know the benefit of rejoicing for another....
This lesson must be a pillar in the drills prepared to spread, to reach the dark paths,
The inhabitants of the dirt region travel all too frequently....
Major I believe we are on a mission of redirection…
Certainly an orchestration of truth….

And here dirt region travelers we are beyond the illusions, The profound mysteries of our self identifiers, We have taken birth in our own bodies from the force that gives life to the world in human form. The greatest spiritual teachings, tells us, we are not who we think we are, we are created to express All life possibility...we are all things, to be able to love, to know oneself, To know thyself, But our conscious gets lost in the patterns...And here we give to those the lesson of...The truth or castrated truth....you must by now know that The universal must be wedded to the personal to be fulfilled in our spiritual ….

JS /Ls

Free

By

Lady

Your actions manifest without thought or maybe the levels of poison in your being took over your intelligence...you were totally deaf and partially blind when it came to the affairs of your heart...I realized very early on that you were fragmented and your fragmentation were mutating as the years drift by...I felt sorry for you more than loved you caught in the strength of a sacred cord...head bowed in humility to the ordinances... obedience gave the decree to default from you and their constitution freed me...

I snagged my stocking in your courtyard while you continued a dance you were not mentally capable of keeping fresh....I broke every code you devised proving I knew you much better than your knew yourself...conversations with essence of enlightenment that sailed over your crown less head stymied you as you mocked the dignity of my intelligence...how many times I looked into your vacant eyes and shook my head...

Now my life has taken a turn ...I know it interest your curiosity... had you allowed your natural and cultivated growth to come together forming an interesting picture of your life you would completely understand my evolving lectures...even as I write this ...if ever you see the words of my short summation...it would still prove foreign to you...I hate unnecessary competition...in intimate relationships this is a killer and very unnecessary...

I can only pray for you ...as I remain free...

Ls

©

Grand Manifestations 11082015

Lady ©

Standing close to you as we waited for various movements in our moment enjoying street manipulations to satisfy artistic swirls satiating your mind I smiled warmth that poured over the area as passing love agreed ...I often hear the extra audible sweetly I hear, confirming the fragrance of beauty sweetly filling the air when our shared aura is present ...the gentleman with my beaded affair gentlemanly applied himself to me as he passed to me my luxury keepsake... as my thoughts stroke sensitive folds of my heart, longing to be in your arms captures me as tears sting the corners of my eyes threatening to spill over...

Funny in this I hear your caressing voice speak into the drift of winds using its motion to message my heart sending choruses of love wrapping intimacy around my soul as if your hands massaged your love into every fiber of my body ... for in the moment of our mental connection a calming peace entered my atmosphere enveloping me as your soul willed for me soothing peace ... in the upward draft I sent a rainbow of kisses scented with lavender satin hugs in rosy ambrosia returning love from the core of my soul ...I know you feel it...thank you baby ...

Ls

©

Halls

Venturing into my mental halls of conscious intellect...I felt

The energy of his intellectual climate...

I rose above the misty trees of verbal leaves and walked on his elegant clouds of senior level professorship...

Can there be magic in these moments? Not at all...

Lavish garments of verbal beauty be this layer...

Gold and diamond trimmed from the far east with the cosmic

Direction of the faithful foundation...

The aura of your cosmic Temple released a palatial decree ... ringing the joy bells in my open heart...

The significant touch of your gentle hand, carries me into your golden soul...

Where the rich of your patient columns orates the intelligentsia, and wise of your master metaphoric vocabulary...

I luxury my mind with each phrase of impartation of the artifacts...

Of his Natural Mental Museum...

The quiet of my attention absorbs the magnitude of spilled gems from the lips of your know...

Then the panorama delight from the edge of your garden of a

Second enlightenment... from the pages of substance out of

His treasure of mental wealth... encouraged my heart...as I function in concert with you on

Elevated levels of awareness...

                    Deep Thought   Ls ©

He Gave A Smiling Nod....06152015 ©

Lady ©

Was this easy for you ...you gave the approving nod and smile... maybe the ease stems from your physical absence...

Is he the one...baby... I already know...

The hall of mirrors reflected the wide continent of his intelligentsia as it spilled into the oceans of his wisdom ... washing the shores with influenced foundations of truth ...

To the acute of hearing... and the advent seekers...

I knew it was him before your awaited nod of smiling approval...

My other observation was the dignitas of his moral character... for sure the rudiment of him I've been privileged to acquaint with as I leisurely referenced his moral psychology from the inlaid chapters he carries deep in his side... and found the pillar firm and just...

The middle village was his proving ground ...as the structures of his enormous formed at the feet of his Gamaliel ...east of the garden ...under the willow of the Bohdi near the winds of Sinhalese...there the mastery was imparted sanctifying the message from the foundation ...making the combinations palatable to the masses...

I saw a great and ugly beast use the cloak of night to devour the instructions of the guided prophet ...he feared not the controlling spirit of the foul beast and continued the much needed journey ...

The text of his language re formulated his science and gained technical knowledge ...his wisdom calculations modulated as like the changes that regulate the music of a beautiful song...I heard his thoughts echo in his library and prepared to assist in the trod...on the ring I saw a golden key ...representing this is legal and regal ...As he gave a smiling nod...

Ls

He Took Me Higher

Lady

Studying the strokes of my pen brought interesting flow to my engaged mind...wisdom spoke in clarity as my sponge of interest absorbed the content of his delivery... he took me with his leading hand and stepped on an atmospheric cloud moving toward The Great Citadel

Stepping into the outer court I shroud my head for my following progression would stand me in the Holy Place where in my higher conscious of meditation met with the voice of Holy Wisdom...clear from the court of His assembly I saw him say write it down and make it plain...he spoke in fluent tongues of multiple languages at once sending tear stained pages to the 7 churches of Asia again and many times again as their repetitious orating of His sacred Words beat in rhythms of ritualistic rhetoric lacking His warning...I heard and felt His message...I spread my pages to follow in my heart (mind) the urgency of Revelation I found in my youth

more focal than the Genesis of time walking to Eternity...

For awareness has broadened and bridged my knowledge and increased my desire for truth no chaser...He opened with His introduction as recorded by prophetic witness...without hesitation He roll called the regional bodies and clearly addressed the angel of the associated body...clarity jot on my mental pages...my mental fingers turned to Ezekiel 3: 17-20 for the words rose in my ear...angel, son of man you were made watchman and you gave not heed to my warning their blood I hold you accountable for...He raised His voice placing emphasis on His intolerance saying, " you tolerate the spirit of Jezebel misleading them into sexual immorality and the eating of foods sacrificed to idols"...careful what and whom words you eat ... then his voice rose again to the second house and the angel saying, " wake up you have a reputation of being alive yet you are dead"...he reminded them he held the seven spirits and seven stars (seven major Chakars) so plain if you study the sacred way... I heard him voice to Ephesus how faithful she was but had fallen from height (consciousness) and forsaken her first love...for this He will remove them (destruction) if they repent not...

I was held in a place to study what was again given to me on a level above the last ....

Now the voice soften to Smyrna saying, He sees the injustice and her poverty admonishing her to fear not the synagogue of satan occupied by they which are false...He said in you rest overcoming power...let him that have an ear hear the Spirit of God speaking to the Churches...then to Pergamum He said, "I know that you live where Satan has his throne yet you remain true to My teachings but there are those among you who listen to the teachings of false prophets who are corrupt leaders, teachers and preachers leading people into fatal compromise with worldliness, immorality and false ideologies all for the sake of personal advancement and monetary gain" He stood lengthy as he spoke far above a whisper calling them to repent... Sardis He warned to wake up to truth and obey or die in your ignorance...

"Philadelphia", He cried I have placed before you an open door no man can shut ...for keeping His sacred word and patiently enduring …God would be with us and keep us from the hour of trial assurance in God's favor …

Now to the angel and house of Laodicea He would they were hot or cold but since they were lukewarm he is about to spit them from His mouth if they didn't repent receiving His gold where in lay no corruption along with garment to cover their shameful nakedness(cloaked in his sacred word) ….He stands at your door of elevated consciousness let him in and He will teach you from His sacred geometrics and Holy Words…

Ls

Her Verbal Pen 09302015

Lady©

In your absence my verbal arrangements orchestrated a strict mental hold on my pen, sweet ink my friend… for you see as I reminisce of our articulated cosmic energy shared with streams and strokes of produced magnificent originals, I hear my soul whisper in echo how she feels my void, I miss you …awe love my sleeping hours are filled with your intensity such that I awaken reaching for you…my waking hours are spent reliving our life moments …I pen my lines of dear from my erected temple in the heart of my soul…

For my orbits and intersects of spheres in the milestones of my human time, among all that I have encountered, is so delinquently inadequate compared to a few moments of we bliss as we journey watching the world turn…we have not to ever search for tomorrow

The days of our lives have always been …Father knew the beginning from the end and planted us in step with His divine wisdom …

My beautiful Darling holder of my opposite as I surrender to your authority knowing in our human society, perfection is not goal driven but maintaining consistency is our desired perfection…

Angelic confirmation among several distortions and distractions keep me grounded and certain ... for I am sure of your distinguished prompts as I sensually awakened to your scent you rubbed deep into the pulse of my soul revealing your validity in our today ...I hold my quiet vision, for I know where you lodged until clarity revealed your posture ...I have always loved you from my treasure... my thoughts send shivers of delight over my mortal being...how lofty these feelings that will climate an intimate concerto as we play our harmony unregulated no time distinctions just the smooth warm tender of our love...

I know love from my wet house... she has been my whole friend she would never fragment my adornment she keeps me with her wealthy essence ...I share my verbal swing with you my love... how pure you rest in my garden as I yield to you in our combined victory ...the vines of my heart have interlocked with yours ...if we pull away...

Ls

High Levels 10192015

Lady ©

ENGAGING in mental communing as our oceans blend

Together as an isthmus allows two bodies of the same water connect and flow inside around licking each others water lines laughing and frothing inside of our natural existence... for my physical was in multi multiplied tasking ... energetic and harmoniously moving in my forward not ever moving you from our place... stroking you with adoration that encouraged your soul as you returned the energy blending us on a balanced frequency as we settled in comfortably with knowing... holding hands viewing our open door...

I find words to describe you and my feelings inadequate when my heart is beating in your rhythm as you regulate it so that I'm experiencing you as we enter the first door moving in a spiritual glide approaching the turn for the second and third doors...

Your concentrated solution shared with my higher awareness enriches and calibrates my knowledge bearing wisdom reaching deep into before there is...as I stated our frequent and known vocabulary, is not potent enough to adorn him as I see him... when in this mental vehicle with you I hear the sounds of a heavenly utterance that speaks the purity of our dominate third eye ...you knew before my prescribed entry...how exciting that was... for when the right angle of my vision allowed your total entry, my elation too engage in thought with one who is sent delighted the free structures of her mortal sensations ...I still delight in knowledge of sanctified surety for I smile continuously as my beam radiates contagious electrodes that smiles even a strangers steely countenance...

Being with you has drawn me into levels of elevated authoritative awareness culminating and repeating the process effortlessly over again ...

What an awesome vision you have become...you knew all the time ...

Ls

©

Higher Thought

Lady©

I thought about you today knowing I would enter and meet you in the fourth dimension feeling your gravity encouraging me to step into the fifth with you... known results are an abstraction that occurs in mathematics where it is a legal construction explained to me from the documents of his scientific oracle... then to venture with him serves to increase my spiritual awareness...

We are physical beings having reached a conscious connective level of agreement possibly forgotten during our water entry or maybe not... awakened having moved frequently steeping thru dimensions increasing our spiritual harmony as we seek to absorb every particle to bring light and truth into darkness...

I affectionately refer to you... respecting your Kingly helm...I slipped in my haste to share a thought... challenging my position I rehearsed to you my salutatory address which had a brief serenade...when the students ears are ready to hear then comes the lips to fill them with wisdom...I long for the wisdom of your star travel which glide a bit far...I hold the secure of your garment in my right as I read your lines in my left...

I keep his mathematical portions in his apron close to me for review...the charts read to study to show my approval

I saw cosmic dust in your hair as if your last travel bore yet another anointing...joy spoke in my soul as I stayed close anxious to receive an increased understanding of your prophetic customs as you laid mental ground work involving researching techniques that included inverted geometric forms...how even these are in harmony with Divine division that created the universe....

Ls

How Do I Sisterhood With You… 04302015 ©

By

Lady

Strange at times…others completely perplexed…

Love of my self is not an ego trip …I learned to increase in positivity and for the sake of balance and order turn the negativity down…at all times…

I'm never a victim when it comes to your miss management of your outpouring…there by signifying clearly why the reins of maturity has placed a bridle on my sisterhood mare …it's almost impossible to ride with you…

At eight I wanted to be your friend and you chose to alter the characteristics of my new dress and found it funny …even at that young age I knew something was wrong with the process of thought that entangled the webs of horror imaginations floating in your shifted crown…

How Do I Sisterhood With You?

I loved you way into adulthood and watched you fumble and error with the choice of loves…I listened to tales that curled the hair of my mind to know you had endured the lack of love in your life at the hands of some cruel sadistic maniac that silenced one or two of you permanently...I think about you and my heart hurts for you...

What was also so tangled... the conversations you wanted to drag me into talking ill of another sister ...my reluctance to engage in that chatter ish... came from my upbringing ... "carry no tales and watch those that do "... was rehearsed in my hearing... I'm quiet you took it to mean I was slow... I cursed a few expletives and you didn't like that from me...you recognized my anger but not my love for you...you stole from me, spilled grape soda on my sofa...your man said then flat you are not a friend but I was a friend to you ...

I said nothing and forgave you...

See now why I prefer to talk to a dude before you...and some of them are not worthy either...

But we are sisters...we should have a strong bond ...when I need to talk...what we discuss should stay with us...not spread far and wide...

This is why I don't confide in you...my husband warned me about you in my youth to never, ever discuss or criticize my man with my sisterhood or any one else for that matter ...you hated me because this man adored me and kept me close to him in his protective care...Why Sister?

He knew you better than me ...my love for you hesitated my hand to embarrass you and call you the retched names most give you ...you never saw me loving you...

How Do I Sisterhood With You

Now we are mature and you do you and I do me...your concern is how much younger I'll look if I dye my hair...you know that's not me ...but you offer suggestions that have no tie to me ...You cry for a sisterhood but you didn't make yourself a righteous sister to cover under

Sisterhood with me...I'm so lovingly hopeful...There now I love you to life ...But...

How DO I SISTERHOOD WITH YOU...?

Ls

©

How It Feels ©

By

Lady

Early you imparted thoughts like a juniper sunrise...with it bore the rays of a verbal trend that kissed my soul...

I can smell your soul's core ...as your lavender articulated your admiration for our unity...

Does the wind manipulate the willow and palm to demonstrate our own strengths...trials cause us to bend ...but the bend strengthens the sustaining muscles ... my arching hurts and I cry to the mercy of this extreme ...you watch to encourage and guard me with protection...

You are so beautiful as your continued oration reinforced the quality of our intimacy that remains with me...you are on my mind without effort ...it's a gratifying pleasure to sink into the secret place of us ...there... never contained an almost ...my inner surrender to you made a complete outward surrender in total visibility... so intense the corners that witness the soulful stems of our love... they questioned if they may have joined a heavenly communication...

A bird shrilled at my door …I opened it to welcome the breeze of your love …he carried a new tune… it had the registers of the many facets of your voice… I'm so consumed with you …you sit over my entire person …have I been endowed to you from a foundational order… I quibble not…

For I know in the inquiry of my smiling heart … without a shadow of a question …!

Ls

©

I feel It All The Time... 03202015 ©

By

Lady

Would or can this be a rebirth of the holly of my thoughts that merged so wealthy and true...at the fire of invited time...I'm intoxicated although sober...over tones so refreshing in my spirit...

I sought another positive vibe to extinguish some rancid taste fallen into in your beautiful mouth ...

I chalked myself and then rose high above the outline to analyze my seemingly distorted position...

My curls blew in the sweet breeze as my heart shaped her own vivid reinforcement...were you surprised I stayed clear of your tangled path? Peace and goodwill Shepherd my vision ...

In the twilight I glimpsed a harvest containing the bottom of the last hill not mentioned in the text yet...

I built my temple from the basement up...from the measurement installed in my memory...

The cornerstone was dutifully inscribed

No More...She feels it all the time...!

Ls ©

I Hear His Voice

By

Lady

YOUR VOICE ushered truth...rushing past the bow of any mitigation... you bathed my mind with golden floral scented with wisdom absent of any arrogance...our sacred holiday in titillating verbal rhapsodies refined in total elegance not born of these present constellations...propagated from the foundation... taught from the lips of the triangle...experienced in the margin of time...

Where in could I be in solo? From the halls of your communication...I knew these be many entries of many that you would facilitate my focused attention...It has passed many revolutions with me in control...the visitations from your rule were so many if this be not... then cosmic energy be in a faulty cycle...

I looked into a passing window... you realize my sensitivity far exceeds the tenants of the common era as do yours...the digital stratum forming the information of our why connections formed a line of the same magnitude in a similar crossing... logic can't explain what just is...

Your claim on that part of me was authoritative full of confidence...but then your confidence is key in our loving abundance...I leave it to you...and smile my luxurious heart... shinning gold over your thoughts as we unite in mental conversations taking us deeper in universal understanding...

Your soul's revenue refutes depletion...your extended open hand...gives as well as receives...sitting in perfect mathematics dividing the syllables of truth...

My answered prayers as I walk with you in organized chapters promoting healing and wisdom...

Ls

©

Cosmic High 06192015 ©

By

Lady of Love

Mentally dancing in the mist of our love…breathing the cosmic winds…who, what and ever matters not in this place…we are the only here …for in the time this particular house rules… awe you know…we have been in this age for a number of years …. on the 5th me and you on the 6th … I waited for you to tour in … observing how we fell in step with prepared harmony… I smile now in the beauty of it all…your measure of calm I so admire …I smile to myself… my infra red pulled you into view as the tailwinds of a discarded mystery drift far into space …

As I traveled I felt without you traveler …and when I examined the close of many contacts I realize how long your existence has been with me …

Circulating in the tenants of truth are the sincere pillars reinforced with the mighty strength of integrity…it is our strong cable… e'en as we trialed for a stable place among the unenlightened…now… clarity has become my vision …as you speak from the keys of wisdom…my soul nudges my core in multiple patterns of agreement… as the oration brings the challenge to tailor the message for my express use…

My inquisitive nature will overturn hills and uproot valleys to obtain fruitful paths in my forward ...the general of your dissertations do bear witness to the harmony of my foundation... moreover his intellectual dignitas is outstanding... with an easy mental cord to follow...I found myself smiling...as each presentation issues a golden key... always studying ...a true workman not ashamed... truth is the unknown in many convoluting equations...

Ls

In My Soul ©

By Lady

From the swing of my soul …I felt you as your will brought you into my atmosphere …as your honorable presences imparted the literary of your legitimacy…I wept in gratitude as the darling in verbal harmony confirmed the witness of my spirit…

This kingly man approached me with meditation in his crown as he imparted scented blossoms of his mental apex…

He imparted in my soul's hearing, the first six chapters of Solomon's memoirs in a few minutes… so careful to encourage my further understanding for absorbing his museum …

We held the hands of our souls as we exchanged verbs that leveled the foundation of doubt …

The beauty of his map intrigued and comforted me …my heart whispered as my attention sharpened to gather all in this love … I hung on to the jewels of his generous conversation …the cosmic connection was the thread from a distant planet where the witness of him was planted in my spirit…

This verbal dignitary positioned me to receive impartation of a mixed variety to secure our love…

The eyes of the fence of control was broken as he entered my atmosphere …

I unite my full soul to the full of his soul ,,,embraced in a system of Universal strengths committed to the wise of this love with positive depositions from our souls…

LS

©

Intelligence Is Spiritual 06232015

By

Lady

The magnificent highway used for his potent verbal delivery... bringing wisdom in waves of wind... paved with golden syllables...diamond etched in verbal fire...lead me to a spiritual attention reception as the gold was selflessly laid before the bishop of my thoughts...

My ear gravitated to his voice ... opening wide to sip the pertinent logic of each captivating syllable...she opened the royal folder passed to her from the distant before there was time...balancing his verbal flow as he taught...she energetically connecting... researching even her own thought... waging intelligent dialog with the volumes of his library...teachings bound in ancient wise ...passed to him in a quiet field...

Heavy laden with understanding as information passed the test...

My spirit received his open freedom as he placed metaphoric understanding on the four corners of my soul...introducing me to a deeper pattern commuted by his sensitive delivery...my researching allowed for my quick absorbing understanding as I stood in the center of his awesome Citadel...the volume of his oration was given to my ear as a soothe like the application of a herbal lotion ...both healing and restoring ...

This awesome warrior gave her mental combinations...discussed in mathematical patterns of logic ...adjusting the tenants of the previous institution... making for clearer understanding ...what may have been complex now stood complete as he poured worlds of reasoning into the sound foundation of my receptors...

Every word was ever palatable to and for my mental digestion ... I sat at his feet in awe...his un divided attention

Taught now from the scrolls in the pouch he wore in the qualifying auditorium of higher enlightenment ...at that presences he selected her to study with him ...the preparation brought us to an astrological alignment...the spiritual agreement brought us to many spiritual powers...

Class without end ...in his and her sleep his telepathic communication feeds her substance for her enrichment which must be shared in her assigned region... his philosophy Is spIrIt agreement as his spiritual conduct guides her hand ...

Intelligence is deeply spiritual...

Ls

©

Over this Trod
By Lady / Jeffery

We sailed thru the storm …the flowery beds were never easy The thorn of rose often pricked the top layer above our sinew My eyes blinked at the stabs…oh how Nobel your guiding hand When my heart would demand I stand and trample the Bush shedding her in her withered hour…Oh precious is My love …

I knew the wild berries we could eat, wrap your hands in several layers of her pink moisture, Thyself my guide and Stay can be, Where nevermore your eyes may look on me Our strength and resilience demands a commitment to our values Even though, I will stand with you wholly on the above statement, Any American who claims to love this nation with all his or her heart should take the same view.

You dined under the wisdom tree…gathered the much envied Syrupy bark…gird the leaves of wisdom around your waist brought with you all the nutrients from the Barky tree…the fine elixir mixed with truth, wisdom, understanding And love, proved for some to be strong in taste…oh my if they Had read the whole book they would partake and refill …

Yet you have come too dine at wisdom's bar and cafe patio under the cool canopy of his mental retreat, come and arrive in his flow in the deeper layers underneath his bark. Allow him to the feeding of her nutritious diet that to will pass on vital nutrients to his reptile. to sit indulgent, and with him partake to him to encourage your inner child to fill in the blank…will she allow stirring of remnant with a smooth sweet liniment….

There is a remnant at the turn of the second wooded lane

Awaits the word of the angels wing…the perfumed garden
Of a rainbow mix…blend their hands to open palms
Receiving the harvest from afar… The pine bush bloomed
on the snowy trail…I warmed your feet In the pocket of my
soul…you smiled as the journey Moved from garden to hill
…

She came like the fountain of rainbow dawn from the obscure heart of night: Like the water of water, within which was her melted of inner body sugar and the essence of roses mixed; She worked her hands like a primitive fire drill by rubbing palms of both her hands swiftly together, making fist tools, for her meat grabbing harvesting and reached inside his zipper dwelling of his close earth, she was the last of her species and knew how to fondle her way into his heart.

There sits a man who pointed the more our way… I thought but never asked do we capture from the Valley that wasted away …or is the trod To breath the truth over the mental barren land … Your wise wakes the sleeping daffodils by the Edge of the clearing …they wait for amazing In the waters from your belly well\ I love the truth of you in numbers …the music of Your intellect can not be stilled… notes ring in the mind Of my complete sterling free…!

Though wise men at their stage beyond adolescence, know light is right, richest in bounty and in beauty clear, Yet the Man would at once run for your heart; lost within her, the wake of The Passionate Sportsman and his friend, Bound by age, comfort and zest, The inquiring hand could not rest… by the water's edge, and save for that—daffodils. It's recognition of what is unfolding everywhere, every moment, with you. It is felt as you realize this has nothing to do with external things, like physical appearance, perceived, I am a part of all that I have met. The energy of the mind is the essence of life. Knowing yourself is the beginning of all wisdom, that's how, we me and you, found us….!

Ls/Js
©
102314

Knowledge In His Halls

By

Lady

From his immaculate halls, flowed rivers of verbal encyclopedias ...

I stood on the shore of his mind to await the EBB TIDE of delivery

That would favorably wet the feet of my thought ...

Reception of knowledge rises from level to level ... Inside of the mental

Construction, of solidified shelves bearing information in my minds library catalog ...

Canvassing the illustrious magnitude of his flowing cosmic tenants ... I received a significant deposit adding substance to the sorting binds in my library dynamics ...inviting for suitability in mental partnership with his halls ...

Lovingly I refer to him as scientific ...for the science of his selections brings favorable matter

Controlled by wisdom in gaining heights... As he develops himself

With the continuum of sought knowledge in abundance ...!

Ls

Natural Queen
Lady ©

She, created in you for you…captivating ingenuity of your desired design…her mental ocean depth un measurable complimenting his integrating flow of mental mathematics forming joining seas…artistic melodies blended in her voice, mixed with a variety of inflections delighting the sensitive fibers of his ear… sculptured image from his dreams…she walked into his vision, Queen, stately ….selection of alluring scents adorning her like veils of silken perfumed air... speaking worlds of wisdom un taught by human intellect…a philosophical scholar imbued from a Spiritual realm not fashioned with human concepts… esoteric knowledge of exchange flowing… eastern wind accepting as he sat with her company mesmerized with her verbal length… intrigued by her surrounding cities of wisdom as they ventured joining their kingdoms of intellectual wealth…

She mirrored his exact moment conveyed as his eyes followed her interpretations expeditiously compiled of wise construct from his potent introduction circulating opening letters of his verse responding with confident connective information enveloping some of his structured phrases with powerful sentences of experiential understanding …

He presented me with baby rose buds from a distant garden amidst fields of exotic gardens choosing the summer mixture representing my gentle love for him so strong, embellished with his signature compliment reading, "my Darling"… for our understanding he referenced me, his eternal companion…
I opened the lips of my heart and spoke to his Kingly soul adoring him sitting in his shade created for this dove hour …we scented our beautiful hands with henna spreading lavish sweet streaks in our hair…kissing the crown of his

head filling my sensations with our unforgettable history.... He opened his robes revealing in a small pocket a blue gem we named her sapphire for she shown her astonishing azure blue taking my breath away as her sparkle became my smile …Sapphire's shimmering brilliance captivated my desire to place her with your golden frame and five diamonds…I did …

I mixed saffron with olive oil to massage my King's tired limbs as he cultivated my eager awaiting with consonants of sacred arrangements forming elevated awareness she aggressively embraced…I looked deep into his beautiful and coupled our hands taking in his delightful with kisses surrounding his soul with Queen precious from the heavens of my soul while attending and grooming my yielding heart occupying my eyes… satiating him from loves collection of fruity charm as she delights him with her feminine surrender…who can know the depth of her love for her King…? Love can….

Ls
©

Next Time …Give 04022015

By

Lady

I saw things in you that failed to reveal themselves to you …or you were blind to yourself about yourself… How does one possess a quality in their person and not recognize the essence for themselves…in your particular case you message your conscious mind from the well of thought that is cradled in lies stored deep in your sub conscious mental attitude…

Passionately you tricked your mind to fight against it's self… mental incarceration by self…

You've waved thru partial development crutching with silence… quiet has been your dependable ally…agreement to this dimness a second…

I remember my own awakening to knowing you better than you knew yourself…now I understand the fear behind your gaze… the distant porch of your persona for fear of being uncovered… perhaps if the total fragments of you had been presented in humility… I could have helped you mend the fabric with love… the lies alone hung a noose around

Love's neck …this is what you can't figure out…

You left love to die…her mind was not tied and she freed her body…

You saw love in full ...you are aware now... but you missed that light and flight ... maybe now you will be able to give love to another as I did you...

Ls

©

Not A Minute More!

By Lois Shaw aka Lady of Love

The day has passed and gone
The evening shades appear;
O may we all remember well
The night of death draws near
John Leland

You tried me for the last time
Thinking I could have a life with you
Being with you is like serving time
I had to fast get off this horse ish grind
I must have been out of my mine
I have closed the curtains changed the locks
Shampooed my carpet, threw out all your stuff
Including your ugly socks

I have dust my house of your finger prints
Moving traces of you is my driven intent.
I want nothing of you left to disturb my peace
Don't question me about your nasty jar of funky hair grease.

I need to sue your hips in court
Wasting my time and energy on you like it was a new sport.
I am sure the judge would see it my way
And tell the bailiff to remand you cause we all know you can't pay.

I'm a nice person and like to on purpose be like that
I should have known better just by how you sport that hair-do
You were no class and certainly all whack.

You are so confused, look up and watch your step, you could slip
And fall addressing yourself to live permanently down below.

I have witness to you time and time again,
Tried to show you that path you're following is a horrible sin
You laughed and poked fun at living right, now look at you umm
Boy is you some sight!
What horror shows must go on inside your dark depraved mine
Fairy tales and man tales every dumb thing of it's kind.
But I shall not spend another minute with you
I promise you cat daddy I'm done and O! so damn through!!!

Now you charge me with a crime against love, what are you drinking
What were you thinking when your were out there freaking
And I was peaceful as a heavenly dove
Lord, please send me help from above.

Tighten up, keep your paints on, close your mouth
Let dignity form.

That's right I said it not on minute more
Will I tolerate my love treated like its stuck in a revolving door
You can fantasize all you want about my style and faith
But this one thing is for sure
If my hope and faith were not in Jesus blood … Trust me
Your blood would have left your body awhile ago
Like waters with out warning how it spills all over the

floor.

Man step on and please leave me alone
Stop talking to me on paper and refrain from using that phone
Your conduct is not acceptable in the presence of a Queen
Turn and walk away you need to become unseen!
Maybe you will learn to live in God's order
Stop fighting Divine order and clear your head
Before you wake up and find you self cold and dead.

LS/ aka Lof L
   ©
4/9/14

On Destiny Road 111314
By
Lady

In my travels I met a certain man ... We talked for there was a walk to accomplish to reach the same destination ...
I believe he was sent to impart a confirmation ...
As we walked he engaged his
Mental briefly to pay a compliment and then imparted wisdom in duality...

The second impartation stood up in my spirit on this morning causing serious alarm ... I had dismissed all of him or so I thought UNTILL the audio touched my mental ear afresh ...the warning fence read ... Warning Guard
Your Mind Against Mental Thieves ...Wow
The parable of the Good Samaritan visited my conscious
My pen is the door to the expressions of my heart ...
Or to keep it known, my mind...
Do I express my thoughts and count it joy when they comfort those that wish to try them on and do?
I must array in Ninja thought and grid myself against
What is pinched without conscious consideration...
On Spiritual Warfare Duty Now...!
Have a blessed Day ...
Continue to Love
Lady ...!

Ls

A Breeze © 03112015

By

Lady

He stood at the open gate of my mind...in bold

Fit...not without reason... for his posture was legal...My smile broaden as his mental embroidered a new thread with gold that crowned my thoughts...

His articulation carried the honor of ancient knowledge that transferred a weight of exchange to my soul ...

We prepared a table with only two seats adorned with

Pour in our shared challis ...

How gracious were the pinned notes imparted by him at our general conception...there carried a seed I responded with a name for the sake of our precious bond, I call her Upper New Level...

As I walked this step with him ...the chorus sang a tune that resounds off the hallowed halls...as his words placed complete logic across my conscious table...

My pen draws the ink that illuminates my thought

As the print of his words create a filled canvass over and over again...in A Cosmic Breeze...

Ls

©

Beauty is Her Thought

Lady © 07182015

WAS IT THOUGHT that brought me to the edge of you enticing manifested dreams...the pull is a desirous tug...I gave into each nudging beauty of his male-nificent charm...there be not a string of strange leading me deeper into his passages ...agreeing with the spring leaves adorning the outer triangle of her pretty garden...

His eyes pierced my heart...in high confidence... he knew they did...giving his significant surety as he allowed his brown gaze to linger deep in the windows of my soul....my almond purity drank her mortal fill of him in those moments...still she begs for more like she is in a drought as she visits the harvest of him...I love you... rare beauty...I stand in the loft of my security as he sends his breeze... he knows I know the scent of his wInd...we organized the strain from the foundation... accepting the return be late...executed with regal quality for the etching of regal crowns...

She listened to the echo of his heart as the reverberation stoked a well flame...embers burn eternally for them....I knew the moment of inception he is...I vibe so pure in the secret quarters of our sanctuary with him...as we reinforce the bare thread of our charts...we came together in the wholeness of love ... the delirious delight of his being trembles my flesh...the result of absolute real... my mind walks in deep thought and harmony with my love...this love grows from a spiritual cultivation...not by the hands of flesh ....so so we were near for many revolutions as we orbited near and then here....as my thought embraces your captivating beauty...

Ls

Eternal Love

By

Lady of Love

    Felt your flame spread today...cosmic mental linked at destination un planed ...it's
Destiny routed ... The sweetness of your entries in my spirit exceed the treasures
Of King Tut ... The regal adoption of my heart has turned my path to streams
Of life flowing tenderness... My image is powerful of you...Never in a million skylark journeys could I have mentally constructed a love eternal
Like you...
    My physical posture adores you…
But my witness to you, tunnels deeper than sensual acknowledgment …
Physical ... I love it too but that's such a small part of you ... so private and protected ... I smile when I think venture ...
Damn ...Darling love I fall in love with you and your distribution of instructions and advise ... Sweetheart from the region of precise understanding and unwavering combinations of concern righteously urging me forward ...
The seat of my loves intelligence, Powers his forward motion and wisdom is his constant enlightenment beam... his journey orchestrated at his second return…
Your divine overlay is God fashioned for this life journey...

    I touched many sacred articles that enlightened and broadened my spiritual sight… bringing me to fuller understandings of mysteries hidden in life… some awkward turns I mastered with your guidance many executed alone on my journey ahead of you which produced silence necessary for my strength… I sang the words of Psalms 121 which hymned the origin of both our strength….

He whispered several times high into the atmospheric dimension of the fourth where interference is not lawful… "I always have your hand physically and spiritually" ….I smelled a yield of jasmine sprinkled with myrrh limning the breath of his verbal sacrifice… this I received as lesson to tuck in my awarded apron…

We finished the chronicle application set for memory infusions that I would take on a mission I would organize and distribute on my own ….Excited to have rendezvous with he that lingered in my spiritual sight in length …now allowing manifestation of partial flesh appear…to see and touch whole of him knowing there remains that which must wait but yet is here could be complicated to third dimensional thought to understand…she is in his higher consciousness and he in hers… I launched a cocoon idea and he returned to my soul a distinct yet beautiful butterfly…he streamed sun rays over a field of daffodils for her… opening a new path of knowledge… mist fell from celestial heavens…I recorded on the tablets of my heart all the letters of my witness…his arms of comfort and wisdom surrounded my soul…

Ls

©

Either Is ...This

Lady of Love

Either found us this way...in love...I knew after I hung up from you that this was our way ... the beauty of your expression colored my sensations... the sexy call of your tone spoke in measures my soul confirmed as it allowed my spirit to drink from your amazing wealth ...could it have been either or ...never my love only this...

I felt your soul course my body...igniting sensations as you left your total you in every chamber of my passing blood... resembling a relay race... my smile lit the night in my room as I opened my heart receiving more of him...loving from a purpose patterned with all notches fitting...I love the timing ....

Patience adds life to love ...you have brought me thru world after world of un manipulated understandings...I know you possess a root of majesty...I adore you from an un common elevation... wisdom was added to our girth from Alpha...

Without employing doubtful energy...the natural of my flesh is alive...I see your passionate man...for our we to have only this element in high priority would nullify our mission...

How grand and exquisite our spiritual and natural composition ...as we engage in our scared arenas ...for there are many...your information systems overflow with hope and enlightenment …so important is this information of truth bringing healing to our region …

As we poured into each other during the last transmission as we stepped from a late dinner in a secluded park …my heart wrapped around yours as yours fold over mine…whispering the crystal language of love given to us ages ago…now we must interpret and dialog with and for our beloved region…

I stare into your wise elect declaring not either …only this…

Ls

©

Hear the Truth
by Lady/Jeffery

The lips of your words warmed my soul as you verbally required my understanding to be studious in her reception… Your timely orchestration escorted my mind to a Galaxy of frequent visit…I smiled as your revelation Synchronized my thought with urge of noble persist during My dawning and mid hour… This communication impartation extracted a glean of Immediate identification and admiration The bridge we crossed, moving us to a destination Of expanded understanding of configurations told And explained in regulated intervals by the Ancient of Days, Rest according on my prime seat…

Whatever we have words for; that we have already got.... it was not my lips you kissed, but my soul. ... I think of your arms being around me and cannot express my delight. Remember your word to your servant, for you have given me hope…Sometimes in the way we verbally petition God…wise of knowledge…..

The wise man of your fellowship confirmed of the Secret Place… Our frequent abode of replenish… We supped with him in sagacious divide …my position inclined my ardent ear…

This ancient manuscript has lain hidden for centuries in the vaults of my mental And one may think it is a secret place, but knock upon his door and come across the threshold and come in on the verdant side of the great river, our groundwater is replenished and streams run high, in honor of that supernatural love and joy, with which your

Immaculate Heart was replenished during the abode of your divine garden….

She strung two roses, one violet and two regular leaves… Keeping the number odd and the table even … The valley echoed with the cry of morn… Were we sent to shelter them from a dark mental storm? Seven eagles rest on the right hill waiting to escort us just to the edge … Comfort in the Holy Word we repeated without the cold of reference… it stayed alive for purpose sake deep in the storage of our hearts …

Into the valley early one morning and left his trail in all likely ... a few rods ahead of them, and the valley below echoed with their full-throat-ed cry. The Decurion wings of the small mounted escort spat with advantage and could rest his mount and wait. But it has been well remarked that every reference here…God is not truly sought by the cold researches of the brain: we must seek him… There was a reason for my stern words; this is my advice now. .....
By sheer kindness and the Holy Spirit; with genuine love, speaking the plain….and I smile from a happy heart….

I smiled in anxious knowing for the marvelous of your Presentation from His Blessed Will…poured forth like diamonds from the mines of Catoca, rich in brilliant substance… The purity invoked rejection …a few were willing among… My soul danced as she received the wealth of his patient impart … Mist fell in approval…the air filled with the cleansing flood of Myrrh laced with lily of the valley swirling in dignified streams Surrounding the thought of his accomplish … Oh for a heart to sing …the nightingale spoke her tune He smiled for his message invigorated his own soul And flowed like a river impregnating the lonely shore I pray they now know…

It is a marvelous blessing I hope each of us will recognize and cherish as a gift from God. As she, this song of silence sung, my soul became refined, Or purified, I know not ... And by this she did truth impart, befitting of her station, my soul became as Mist fell in approval… the fairest of all Rivers, loved To blend his murmurs with my Nurse's song, Flowed along my dreams? ... Fair seed-time had my soul, and I grew up ... The mind of Man is framed even like the breath ... Among the hoary mountains; from the Shore

As we walked we came to the tabernacle to rest ... He knew the chambers of, from the diagram of the scroll on his right… We prayed and sought a divine answer ... You penned for me a beautiful song and tucked it close in my hair I wait for the motion of his continues…!

We feel the long pulsation, ebb and flow of endless motion, i with my leaves and songs, trustful, admiration, as a father to his father going. His dream skating towards the desk in Sexalicious slow motion. Oh! 'Behind closed doors' is on! They continued to dance, moving closer with each song, until his.... the moment it's done, i inhale and close my eyes against the truth of it and there she stands.....

Ls/Js

Wake up Shake up

By Lady

When the attacks are frequent and intense...rest assure deliverance is nigh The adversary is trying to keep you from your blessing If he can sway you ...delay is evident...stay watchful You say deliverance...? Like you are foreign to trials When they come in like a flood know you must be doing something right. Or on the other hand your clam may be disturbed because you are needed to For work on the highway of life... if already at work the interference is to hopefully abort You mission... Lady of Love As meditation counseled my attentive spirit...I felt another presence Trying to intrude...I have encountered this foul presence at another time The point of my first release...He brought with him the spirit of detriment I fought the good fight and prevailed... the strong hold was broken The weaponry I use is not carnal but mighty through God...to the pulling Down of strong holds Did he forget he has been defeated I remained calm... armed in my defense I could use him but there is no time to summon for his help This fight must be fought now... Armed and extremely dangerous So real are the road blocks ...they are designed to turn your attention Away from your destiny...and use you in the process hoping to take Your life before you realize what is going on One undeniable sign is convoluted chatter...switching lanes Between maybe you should or shouldn't and back again Tempered with a parade of subjects...changing your mind Like a ball on the roulette table... Guard you heart (mind) with all diligence... I stand before you not to display any accolades to define myself Nor lend charts to where I have on earth been My very testimony tells who and what I am...Tried in the fire On a mission to spread the good news... And to herald the warning... We sit in audiences listening to uninformed rhetoric... Half of what comes across the podium are half truths and puffed up stories Of over worked imaginations...or the misinformation is intentionally Delivered to keep the plates full and running over... I employ you to study for yourself...to show yourself approved A workman not a shamed rightly dividing the word of truth Pimps and hustlers in the pulpit...you were suppose to use Those organizational skills to support the communities you minister to... Why is Mother Jones without lights this week...I'm sure the price Of her lights was in the plate on Sunday...Monday her service should Have been restored... The word said bring your offering to the store house where there will be substance For the needs of the people when applicable Who visited Brother Jesse...he's been in the nursing home for years now Out of site out of mind....wow Word said I was sick and you visited not...If you did it to one of my least You did it to Me... You bailed you unruly son out of jail...with what monies...you don't work My son is in prison ...you have yet to visit I was in prison and you visited me not...that you've done to one of my least You have done it to Me... My mission is to bring truth and enlightenment to darkness I was lost and now I am found... Let he that have an ear let him hear We are not on our jobs If the ball is dropped we don't have team players willing to hustle to make Up the difference... so sad... I started and I'm going though... May have to go it alone...determined to go through...! 6/11/ 14 Lady of Love c

Mental Seed

By

Lady

His mental gaze penetrated layers of faded moments…resting in the center of her awakened womb…his life force was so potent that she conceived in verbs and adjectives of multiples, maturing becoming her new birth… his molecular structure divided and introduced its self into my life stream as he pulsed his initial phrase causing it to move in precision as he aimed for my now opening portal for reception…

This mental cosmic legend choose to orchestrate and govern the depth and levels he would construct in her minds landscape… for he found solid foundations that would lawfully support his congress of deposits…his movements are smooth as fresh blown glass lending an exciting rhythm to his many modes of distribution… some mental intrusions are not a warm welcome… contrary to that finding this prolific artist's injection are easily received creating ravenous appetites in me …desiring to devour his flowing out pour…

As he prepared a special smorgasbord of his finest delights stimulating thought in her to want more before tasting his immediate preparation… gratitude presented her elegance and I felt blessed that I was his selection to divide his wealth with… information found places to erect headlines in my mental library as he examined and reinforced any missing pages of her chapters... time can fade a page or two he uttered as he gently explained the techniques we would use in his potent delivery of pertinent information for building my mind spans...

Telepathy is one of the many phases of his direct renditions...he addressed my thought and the connection was made flowing in some abstract patterns as he supported his facts...must be a beautiful completion when you observe the growth of your word seed...

Ls

©

Redeemed

By

Lois Shaw

I notice where I stand... I'm always in an orating position ...even If I'm not feeling my usual...
My feelings have zero to do with carrying on my mission ...

I had fainted unless I had believed to see the goodness of The Lord in the land of the living...! PS 27:13
The top of this scripture I stood and recited when God reclaimed me from a life of madness ... There is something deep and important I'm doing and must do and the more perfection my God gives me the more this demon buffs... I can't run from me ... And I stand my ground...and continue my trod...

I feel so alone at times ... But that's when the Master is the lifter of my head and a constant in my ear ... The blessed restorer of my soul...!
Love me in prayer...Redeemed...

Ls

©

—

as he examined and reinforced any missing pages of her chapters... time can fade a page or two he uttered as he gently explained the techniques we would use in his potent delivery of pertinent information for building my mind spans...

Telepathy is one of the many phases of his direct renditions...he addressed my thought and the connection was made flowing in some abstract patterns as he supported his facts...must be a beautiful completion when you observe the growth of your word seed...

Ls

©

Redeemed

By

Lois Shaw

I notice where I stand... I'm always in an orating position ...even If I'm not feeling my usual...
My feelings have zero to do with carrying on my mission ...

I had fainted unless I had believed to see the goodness of The Lord in the land of the living...! PS 27:13
The top of this scripture I stood and recited when God reclaimed me from a life of madness ... There is something deep and important I'm doing and must do and the more perfection my God gives me the more this demon buffs... I can't run from me ... And I stand my ground...and continue my trod...

I feel so alone at times ... But that's when the Master is the lifter of my head and a constant in my ear ... The blessed restorer of my soul...!
Love me in prayer...Redeemed...

Ls

©

—

Positive Thought

By
Lady of Love

In my thoughts rest thoughts ….thoughts born out of other thought
Time gives thought passage to move forward or be deleted…
Some times my thoughts require thought or thoughts to arrange

A specific order of priority and the sequence may change
Depending on the shuffle to honor priority rearranged
Lady

That's He and She complex never complicated…
Different but connected
Complex thinking twins… fitting neat and secure …
Born of different births
Instructed on the Alpha Planet by the Ancient of Days
Prepared for the workings of this awesome time under the Star in the East
He the Star and the Bodhi Tree…absorbing
Engaged in a fight for the minds of the rocked to sleep
Warrior against the trained charlatans of the powerless beast

Lethargic minds miss the point… the beast has no power
You have slept thru the briefing and deployment
You move around in a circle of confusion and intense unrest
Life's vicissitudes have crippled your ability to birth thought
There must be more to this than what I am
Experiencing …should be your cry for deliverance

He has come that you may have life and have it more abundantly
He paved the way with His life
The scrolls are intact for the dirt region …..
You are in the scope of the beasts weapons … they are trained

on you
But he must get permission to use them
Read and research for your self ...Oh inhabitants of the dust
Time draws nigh
The mission is large but there are few workers on the highways and by ways
The inhabitants have been lull to sleep on a false message
We were chosen to bring the message from the teachings of old
The eastern sky has always been the guide
The charting and reading of the sky...a ministry forgotten
But He will bring all things to the knower....soon come!!

Ls

©

Revelation ...08092015

Lady of Love

My praise and devotion went forth...busied myself grooming my Morning Glory...pouring the storage of my heart out spilling the night conversation of my spirit had with The Spirit of God... revelation for my continued journey... a bitter pill for me to swallow that would require me arm myself in four directions as well as protect my heart (mind)....

The first illumination came in answer to my Morning Glory...God is not shouting out of the sky to point our directional way...he is using you and I to get this work done and messages delivered...I received a subtle message that dropped a mega ton of perfect love into my spirit...then confirmed the deposit with a guarantee ...

Between the mixture of joy and love entered love from a far a King bearing gold for me...I knew it to be genuine for the last deposit was far ago ....God used him to bring a healing meditation to His servant...we compared notes and found we were at the same spiritual briefing... the words of his gift poured like a fountain from Glory....palatable is a small representation for the majesty of the connecting realm we ascended to, in a matter of seconds...the force of his guide over stood all I thought I knew...reinforcement with a stern warning shook my foundation as he expressed the effects of walking with blinded eyes...as my rejuvenated spirit lifted her head in great-full praise I wept for myself and others...for the author of this value spoke truth...

He blessed my life with a beautiful closing salutation that brought me to my desk, ink and prayer

Ls

©

Signature Attention...©

By

Lady

I attentively listened to the reverberation of your mastery as it took charge of our we direction...awesome regulator of what could have become a slain tree... the adrenaline flow of the spinning phrases that required prudent stipulation that were not measured... stayed in absolute rhythm according to the applications of his wisdom drips...

When did I discover the fine hairs of his magnetically charged verbosity clamming my inner ear...? I

attended his auditorium and raised high my chorus engaging in separately joined rhythms...

His signature he wore in his capturing stare... I smiled to meet and translate the radiant feeling he was pulsing thru my veins... from many splendor finales ago ...I questioned the rustic chair at the end of his long mental hall... could I or would I leave this elevated landscape that provides the visibility of the mountains east by his planted roots...

We exchanged the ideas resting deep in the folds of proven instruction...I watched as he leveled and balanced the reason of govern taking instruction to new levels as the light of guidance penetrated the pores of a dry land... one captured by malignant adjectives...restoration lived as I celebrated the conquering courtship of his appealing salve...

My scented roses crowned his loyal head as his lips parted establishing direction for stabilization ...we received the parcel of a communing relationship ...decorated in the jewels of mental soul reflections...

Regulation manifest in amalgamation rich ...

Ls 03252015

She Entered His Mental Museum I
By
Lady

Flash of purple flashed in my view …my eyes followed
The flowing trail… hypnotic would be fair in my logic and
My admiration for the color of love…

Grand beauty were the verbal of my thought …my senses
Taste you at the precise moment… you required my
Center seat which is the only you could inhabit in view
Of the total, you bring to my life…
Am I dreaming ..
Or is this the prayer of answer,…his moves are so subtle
Yet I never forgot on the second week, reveal of your
Orchestrated paradise would fit me as you so desired
Was a promise to yourself and me …I smiled it away
For then …you walked me along with you
 hinting all the way …
And then…

Then on recent occasion my drum tantalized with the
Auditory of the strength my mental muscles would be
Receiving from the next interval of structured bridges
Prepared and tailored for me…positive of my reception,
Circumstances danced in accordance to the rhythm of life
Sending me into the museum of your world…
My eyes adjusted and I found silence my companion…
Never a worry the chatter of distract would not find me
here…
My chakars meditation has begun … the flame of desire
Has been lit and the hunger to expand is in process..

To balance the fray I sustained on my journey to the kiss
Of the golden axis, where my rescue and instruction

Met me, with a much needed elixir to fortify my body,
Enabling me to receive, as I entered for frequent
Infusions of required knowledge as inscribed in my soul…

I pushed the heavy door …and entered his royal museum…

I looked in my note charts and started a fresh page
The embedded scribe on the marble wall confused me
For I was entering without you to guide me …it is as though
Your deposits were precise to assist the
 solve of the rudiments
Of my lengthy absorb and for now you are absent…

We do so much together I thought my warrior would be here…
I fear never my weapons are always on lock and loaded…

As I sort the maze of direction one thing for sure…
This banquet of mental concentrate will unify the walk…

Ls
©

The Prophet Spoke

By
Lady

As Morning Crest the sky and Jesus was praised
I slept, not a toss or turn my familiar is one place
A real about Lady…
No dream…The Prophet spoke …the wheel began to turn
Motion was inevitable it was orders of the King
From a distant shore I saw the warn… my knee bent
In an earnest plea…The Prophet spoke…My heart iced
And heated….the lake burst in my head … I pleaded
Inside my silence with the King…ignored the time
That this would bring…
Had I walked in breech…
I cried allowed thrice in vain the Prophet doubled
And came as one…right after the Son lifted the sun
Visions stirred and presented themselves
It was as the Prophet spoke…

Your dirt house is governed by your spirit
Be it The Holy Spirit or an unholy one

He knows the way that I take…He also knows
The detours and delays that my dirt will allow
To come between me and my assignment
He has a way of escape…

How could I have derailed this train of misery
From entering my space
To my warned heart (mind)

The Prophet spoke saying , " no matter what shall be
He has begun a work in you and will keep you
Until the day of Jesus…I cried …I weep now

We are so precious to the King

The Prophet spoke and called me daughter ….a message from
My King …the message sparked hope
The beautiful Prophet continued to anoint my spirit and
The Holy words balm my soul as the oils of The Apocrypha
Sweet Peace flood my soul …I rest in Love

LS/Lol8/28/14

The Tall In Short... 04012015

By

Lady ©

The evening has a beauty that captures me in a sensual swirl ...I smell the rose of you so near...

Is it so far to believe that my mystery is impregnable with thought... ?

The strategic counsel of love guards and guides me ... I can love so far pass yourself ...and be in the next twist in the road to welcome you when you arrive... taking you by the hands of your soul ...speaking energy vibrations to the root of your mental depth... have you experienced her in the citadel of her true...

I come to join the trees of braided wisdom in the park of your soul ... the foundation of your trusting belief was shattered yet not destroyed... I saw a clip of your summer bliss and I know the banquet ...

I felt you open the storage at the center gate ...now be filled...

Ls

©

Sweetly 10102015

Lady of Love ©

Love is Friendship sweetly set ablaze

Sweetly entangled in my thought is you and your handsome pattern... finding me passionately deep in his string of priceless verbal loops ...I smile for I'm so captured ... the forecast of your verbal utterance into the atmosphere has claimed its mark ... you sent it after her knowing the outcome as you sweetly drew her closer to your soul...

I can hear you thoughts in the breeze, feel your warmth as you send portions necessary confirming you feel her too... she drinks your verbal meditations as they stream wisdom's banks ... high in knowledge's tree of ancient didactics... wisdom baptized your wisdom allowing your sharing mechanism to be palatable as well as enjoyable to her...

Remember in late summer she escorted you with less than a tag of persuasion as we closed our eyes an lift high into the stratosphere with angels leading us to that beautiful place lovingly I held you tightly against my heart wrapping you in my soul ...I will always surrender to join you in the splendor of that

Spacious place where we explore extraordinary levels of each other... had this not originated from the altar of our spirits... transcending and shared elevations wouldn't be acquired ...

When you caution me I attend your hidden messages as you send visual lodging it in my place of surety speaking to lofty energy where my baseline understanding lays stimulating growth ....how invigorating I am to him as he watches progression process...for you sweet love I believe you're proud of this accomplishing continuum...

Her company serenaded our hidden we with floral beauty... our tones smiling, we sail on drifts of desired pleasure... welcoming each revolution and dawning that comforts us...I heard your soul sing when you spoke into my heart your love message ...your voice moved to our personal chamber and widened the door bringing me thru with excited measures only we may define... happiness flood my eyes and they brimmed over as my love dried my salty tears with his soft kisses placed gently in his reassuring gathering... producing his expert couturier orchestrated for her comfort position... keeping her lucid for his sweet desired pleasure...

Ls

©

The Whole Seal...03302015

By Lady

I was a bit nervous as we entered the precious place again...Your desire was to sit in the lap of my love and indulge your parched soul while my simplicity adorned your mind with the gifts of my soul...

Our combined aware of what was before royal in our court escalated our second and third discovery of the clear crystal lane ...

Your smile approved the warming quality of this palatial encounter, with no attaching questions...

My focused attention on what continued... infused strength to the large and beautiful climb...

My spirit over stood and your spirit effortlessly joined the meeting ...

Yellow roses were spread along a cordial banquet area... as the hands of our spirit embraced and blessed the secure undertaking...

I poured from the catch at the golden spiritual fountain from the bountiful garden of labor less

Sweet endearment...as streams of wisdom and enrichment came forth that fortified the coming watch...

The prudent and pertinent of the speech of elect was direct and plain ... reference to the tree on each side...

As it's good for the whole to be healed in the mind, body and soul ...healing rich of the leaf ...

Look beyond the seal...

Ls

©

Walk In The Light 08162015

By

Lady

Has your voice become overloaded with words of negativity and you find clouds of despair have partnered as your friend... sometimes the conversations you find yourself dragged into are full of arsenic laden verbs and toxic sentences...silence your voice in the halls of these bitter echoes while yet listening to the draining damage...now tell me in the corridor of confusion where have you found any peace certainly there was no rest... move with me as we create distance between discord and our forward journey...

They tried to drag me into those sort of conferences that net hatred... I saw the look in your eyes when they wanted to speak ill of another as the material they claimed to know was faulty from the beginning to the end of their ugly recitations of half truths and tales puffed up to spark interest in the hearer but this was not a meal for you nor myself

To continue to be part of their berating panel ...I knew we belonged not in this audience and needed to dis associate with the band of protruding ignorance ...I must pass this on to you ... you have the power of life and death in your tongue...your words are seed the universe is fertile and alive to receive that which you say and return it to you multiplied in the interest of your deposit...this life is so mathematical...follow closely...

Our purpose for earth is for the spread of truth... not layering the world with lies and grief...come now my love let's be forever about our Father's affairs...He has given us a mega bank of experience that developed our wisdom and balanced us with understanding ...waste not the wealth of your knowledge, mentally dinning among destruction....we shall lift up our countenance from the shade of dark and watch the witches of darkness flee from the light...I know I saw a few disappear...

Ls ©

Walk On Dust
By
Lady of Love

As I walk in servitude, minding the tenants of my particular
Course, I find my self in the parlor of verbal silence…
Not in a word poor state… but unable to exercise back and
forth dialog
With dust of familiar territory…Alas these feelings
Creep into my conscious mind, delivering illusions of
A many kind…This mental chatter is moving to fast to
identify with any
Suggested path of thought consideration…
I am positive of the originator of this mind strain…
God is a constant help in the time of trouble, I, His beloved
Was being visited by an enemy assignment…
The onset of the attack, God caused sleep to fall upon
My living soul…I rested in undisturbed sleep.

Let me clarify a point that may be an issue.
The state of silence I like, is my call for silence in my life
I felt as though a strange thing had occurred. Of course
I was and am sure I was not in a state of blank for verbiage
Just had no partners to capitulate with so to speak at that
Juncture…
My lost to speak my words, was the enemies forward
signal.
He knows what you like…he is much aware of our
Spots of vulnerability and he will try to fill them
With his agenda… I am a natural orator but choosy with
Whom I passage with…you can't allow every kind
Of watery passage into your inlet…

The enemy is a coward he will attack for sure if you are
alone…
Consider also I was in a bit of an exhausted state
Which provided the rebel a way to lodge an attach on a
Weakened servant of God
This is when my God shut down everything in resting
Sleep…
I dream nothing …not even you …Excellent sign
Given, my past dreams are shoulder taps for me…
When and if I am in dream about a lover…it is usually
To warn about unfaithfulness…remember I expressed
God cares for His servants of serve.
If all is well I dream not …I need to explain that this
Sleep was created for my protection…
The enemy is after my mission and the Spirit of
God is on constant watch over me and He knows what to
do to
Not allow these foul suggestions to creep and nest in my
Psyche
Producing illegitimate mind tenants of an objectionable
kind to
Eat away at the fruit produced over time cultivated…

This I tell you very urgently…you must know
The magnitude of your assignment and be prepared
To go through something…the higher the anointing
The larger the demonic attack…
 I prayed on my awakening …
My pen is my shawl of comfort in this hour…
I care not to say what's next for I already
Feel a preparation in line…
I ink this expulsion almost with tremble
Of hand certainly my heart is steady thanks
To The rock Of Ages…
Personally dust is a bit off beat but spiritually sound…As
 I ink this delivery I can feel the water of sustain

And deep love over taking me…
And I continue my dirt trod… In Jesus Name…!

LS/LoL
8/4/14

If I Were Rich

By
Lady of Love ©

If I were rich, I would be a blessing to those less fortunate than myself.
I would not hesitate to take up the slack in the lives of financially hurting
Individuals and families.
I would pay for items like taxes on an elderly couples homes in jeopardy of being foreclosed on, for taxes. I would purposely go to the supermarket and help individuals

and struggling families with paying for grocery. I would improve shelters and start a
single room occupancy program with the occupants of the shelters. This would entail the homeless renovating old buildings…
making them suitable to live in, giving the disregarded in our society a second dignified chance to live in suitable housing . I would call in markers from my associates generating jobs putting the unemployable to work through on the job training. The Word Of God says you saw me in a bad way and you did nothing. The Word says, if I ignore you and I could have done better by you I'm in trouble with the Lord. If I were rich I would share with Joy in my heart and a smile on my face, making a difference in the lives of my brothers and sisters…!

LS/LoL

4/13/14

Scholar Lois/Jeffery

Intellectual universal scholar

Wisdoms student handpicked of the ancient order before time…

My dear friend…those are big boots to wear For sure, he is in the trenches, attempting to put Out the flames of self and conceptual incarcerations And i understand how to step into the idiotic, the minds Of those who will reject me, but I am an incubus to come Forth, to help end this mental destruction

Covenant keeper of love, truth, peace and freedom, how magnetic are the shared keys… Flowing into the stream of time… Time has given me insight, hindsight and wisdom of the beast He lies in rest and grins at me; I have yet to hurt him But he hears my conjure in the vapors left from the sword No weapon formed against me will prevail…i am dressed with A loud noise of truth… wearing a heavy breastplate of The spiritual divine…i can't walk the walk or the talk as Jesus But sure my walk is of a stand up man… determined.

Waking the masses in hearing attendance I watched as wisdom placed you visible… It was soon pass your last Mahabodhi experience…

Visible is the word, the search for the word and The search for the ultimate truth that many are Alien to, but shall he not be, on the impressive Winding stairway of fifteen steps leading to The porch on the second floor, elaborate and extensive Of an endearing alliance, applied with the experience of The worshipful master…

My inception to that knowledge was very brief ... Providing witness that you were in my orbit soon to appear... Bringing the cable to connect my conscious with lessons taught in the wet house...

His unveiled temple is in the brook of Kidron, The utters of a thing parabolic, his meaning hidden in veiled allegory I am and am not, but is...the sublimist truth and spoken from Given mysteries in the caverns, in the gatherings, hidden in The gems of truth...its provision stated with time....

As time brought you closer to axis interception ... My excitement increased... my audio is sharp... I heard you're nearing steps; the staccato of your gait smiled my heart, to physical joy tears...

Sister, iron sharpens iron; the sanctuary is open to all who pays attention, of those who listen with the understanding that wisdom is gained in the yards of the world and sometimes give to those who have yet Acquaintance of heart and conscience of their own alter... See, I am the product of my deeds...happily I swing my arms with praise of the mighty high

The swing of your arms I saw in my infrared vision... What an awesome warrior were my thoughts... The actual... I knew our work would connect in unity... This mission will not abort...

Aborted mission are lessons that will arrive to revisit, As a traveler in transient, with no settled answer to the Yet battle ahead, it is likened to a wayfaring man, Who is a representation of the great artery that receives no Blood... time brings wisdom to foresight, the acuity of The widowed son...

Time will bring your middle axis into view... Interception at point will take its place... You carry the keys with pride... Humble is your countenance...love your language Sincerity is your banner...truth is the content of your heart Faithful are your footsteps...

How Real Is

By Lady /Jeffery

The magnificent essence of you visited me in my wet house...the familiar on board my senses waiting for the orbit set in mutual perfection to meet...the electrical magnetic fields of marvelous kind pulled us like the clap of the cymbals in the symphonic orchestra...

She had the best twist on damp waiting for proper classification. Ummm! Baby that on wet was good, but there is also the shock of reality, a sense of 'oh my god, mutually empowered in this case, it is quiet understanding, mutual confidence, it is loyalty effects handclap, champagne bottle, and his un-soften instrument

I smelled the odor of the collected thought as you searched and found only your lips to present to seal the long awaited... your massive frame shroud me and I knew I was in loves care again... we held immediate hands as we did in the spirit long before...you had my instructions in your order i love your obedience and love of alpha... your glance asked if I were ready to journey with you... my accurate follow was my reply I saw the red wind pass and bow his head in acknowledgment of our safe and proper arrive...

The new scentsation in search...Coming to our senses: controls our emotions and behavior as well as basic thought processes. of how these seedlings of love affects caring, while prayer does move the hand of god to do miraculous things we do not have, you were acting rightly and according to your understanding of your directions and orders so that your souls would be sanctified in obedience to the truth and that they be filled with love without partiality, that you would be loving one another I have arrived, to be wrestled with as I think I have a solid prize of Distinct loyalty...still the question is how real is it.....

The loyal assist of the universe prepared A regal road...the path flew her rose of rare... The man we talked about met us and spoke Wisdoms keys in the note of your arched Ear... You pressed a loyal disc I wear... His love floral my mornings with his heart we poured the wine of much intoxication and satisfied the hunger...till...

God has fully revealed this plan by sending us now we have heard enough but in these last days he has spoken to us by a son. us into .... his wisdom speaks thus: man who obviously needs to hear more about the word of wisdom, wise men speak because they have something to say; fools because they have to say something we can easily forgive a child who is afraid of the dark; the real tragedy of life is when men are afraid of the light. pious of the heart, i am lost in a love, so great ... passage of time and the stars, are but what we fantasize ... may your sweet wine daily pour upon my lips and my face and you ask how real.... it's hard to say the matter is an illusion. But maybe it just as real as we think it is in adoration..How real is it....

Precious of my open adore ...your content is not hidden from me ...our day fast approaches... We lose the robin that held our golden string that knit the long promised and six bells Rang... I entered on the fifth day you on the sixth... I carried the balm of mercy and grace and my love came full man... Patience is your middle cord...my ever remind the full is yet to be...the hawk dropped the ring of harvest on the path near the next Trodden land...

My love is wise enough to reach out to you To capture you, prefer not your will to mine, never desire that which I have not desired for you, but that it is me that in not hidden, it is of our grace and favor, and your deserving Strong and content i travel the open road. ..... with stone and roofed with sun, where the days pass one by one not too fast with you if you want to know how to trigger the event, read the pages of how much realer this love can get, how real your heart speaks to your soul, how real your actions have become and the answer shall find you.....so ask yourself, how real is it.....

My gypsy guitar played a sultry tune your instant gathered me near I taste the bud of sweet from my lip to my ear A full of our heart you let me share I love this beautiful Poetry tablet we walk the natural as we were sent Loving...

And I'm going to ask you once again how real is it, is it strange, exclusive or a real creation in your mind...how real is it baby..... How real is it...?

Princess and Prince of the Royal Secret.......

Lady/Jeffery

Now the landscape of her fertile understanding Can be seeded and tended too... His assignment embraced furthering her growth... Qualified to do so ... Because there is no subterfuge Found in his being ... Safe to be her guide... Guiding her with a moral and dignified hand!!

Much in the ritual assumes man immortality And in many specific instances the fundamental Tenets are uttered, if man does not continue to live beyond this life, Much then is meaningless and fraudulent....

The Ancient of Days taught that it is wise for A man (woman) to live such that they leave an inheritance... There by planting life trees that continues to bear fruit... Fruit of knowledge especially the knowledge absorbed and assimilated By the Prince at the southern quadrant facing the eastern star...

And the Princess stands in the door way of The house made with no hands, She comprehends the eternal dwelling place of God and The resurrected and glorified body of her redeeming in her life beyond Her endowment of woman is the products of the creative energy of God and she is the gift from him, whom have Place him in man at the cornerstone facing king Solomon...

The inheritance was secrets told to him and her... He and she were taught to teach..., They knew they would be rejected for the message was not of The common era...the message came from Alpha ...

And given to him the true meaning of I am that I am......
Rendering of the most distinctive and title of Jehovah, God given to Moses and intuitively to I, Regarded with such sacredness and I speak from it without whispering.....

Most assuredly speaking loud and sparing none... The hour of judgment draws nigh... The dragon is waiting to kill those who dare to speak What is written on the great scrolls...? The princess and the prince aware their assignment Can be considered dangerous Have been guided and protected by the eastern star.... They have been kept in a place in plain view Until the engaging hour has fulfilled... the time is at hand to give birth to truth Hidden away for this time...

And should I break the secret inner door, As the mysteries of Gods truth are available to those Who earnestly knock?...So the mysteries of What one may think I be are opened by The proper knock of the inner door, that requires To strive for excellent innocence....Because his apron worn, is made of pure white lambskin...

Yet Prince you have been appointed to bring the message... Crack the door my lord and see if there be any ready to receive You are ordained to where the ephod and bring The message to the dying masses...be not slow in making Truth ring in their cities...this appointment is very serious and With carries consequences for not completing this assignment....

Princess as you well know, I carry with me twenty four seven The emblematic significance of the crown jewel Along with the level of equality, the light of life and The spirit of the lion of the tribe of Judah, How could I not finish the task at hand, when the light of Truth is my guiding hand, the secret has been told long ago When Gods children were in the lion's den, and I once relived it again But in front of me, the successful candidate of admission

Forgive me Prince; my worries precede my thinking considering the intense value of this majestic undertaking.... Yes my lord Judah will go first...our protection is under Divine order... No weapon can penetrate this sacred mission... My position Prince is in total consideration and concern for you On every process and assignment... We have been together since we left the first Galaxy... Whenever you're on a mission away I pray your safe return...it has become habitual and today it escaped my lips...

The bond of eternal love to the vows of the eternal sister By the mystic ties are united with one band, The north side of his exalted throne Like the cornerstone of a great moral spiritual edifice And the principals of the great light and the dignity of character. The necessity of an earthly prince that goes into the sanctuary of the princess. Ls/Js

I have graciously labored in the spirit with each piece presented in "Walking in the Spirit". My assignment was designed by Father the Creator to assist with my spreading love, truth and promoting healing to humanity with the words of my Poetry. I have been touched by my own words when orating the same in poetic settings. My sincere prayer remains constant, that Father continue to use me for His Divine Glory. I'm blessed in my walk to be a blessing in the land. May the first fruits of my gift bring light to the dark establishing balance. The Lord is my light and my salvation; whom shall I fear? the Lord is the strength of my life; of whom shall I be afraid? Psalm 27:1. Lois Shaw

www.ingramcontent.com/pod-product-compliance
Lightning Source LLC
Chambersburg PA
CBHW021153080526
44588CB00008B/318